Henry Ford

Auto Tycoon

Michael Pollard

BLACKBIRCH™
PRESS

THOMSON

GALE

San Diego • Detroit • New York • San Francisco • Cleveland
New Haven, Conn. • Waterville, Maine • London • Munich

LIBRARY OF CONGRESS CATALOGING-IN-PUBLICATION DATA

Pollard, Michael.
  Henry Ford / by Michael Pollard.
     p. cm. — (Giants of American industry)
Summary: A brief biography of Henry Ford, who not only manufactured automobiles but also invented mass production.
Includes bibliographical references and index.
  ISBN 1-4103-0069-2 (hardback : alk. paper)
  1. Ford, Henry, 1863–1947—Juvenile literature. 2. Automobile industry and trade—United States—Biography—Juvenile literature. 3. Automobile engineers—United States—Biography—Juvenile literature. 4. Industrialists—United States—Biography—Juvenile literature. [1. Ford, Henry, 1863–1947. 2. Automobile industry and trade—Biography. 3. Industrialists.] I. Title. II. Series.

  TL140.F6P64 2004
  338.7'6292'092—dc21

                                        2003005141

Printed in China
10 9 8 7 6 5 4 3 2 1

Contents

In September 1908, an advertisement in American newspapers and magazines announced the coming of a new car. The newcomer, the advertisement said, was "powerful, speedy and enduring—a car that looks good and is as good as it looks. Better features or as high-grade materials cannot be found in any other car at any price. A better car is not and cannot be made." The new model, the advertisement continued, was to be sold for $850. This was "several hundred dollars less than the lowest of the rest."

No doubt many readers glanced at the advertisement, smiled at its extravagant claims, and

Previous page: An assembly line quickly turns out modern Ford automobiles. Henry Ford believed that speed and efficiency were keys to success in the car production industry.

Below: The Model T was a runaway success. In the car's nineteen years of production, Henry Ford sold more than fifteen million Model Ts.

turned the page. How could a manufacturer sell a car several hundred dollars cheaper than anyone else and at the same time claim that it was the best on the market? It did not make sense. In any case, most newspaper and magazine readers had never imagined that they could own a car. They still regarded cars as toys for the wealthy, not something the average person could own.

What these readers did not know was that the advertisement heralded at least two revolutions—a revolution in the American, and ultimately the world's, way of life and a revolution in the manufacturing industry. The car in the advertisement—the "Ford Four Cylinder, Twenty Horse Power, Five Passenger Touring Car"—was the Model T. It was a car that would change the world, and it was the brainchild of Henry Ford.

A car for the multitude

The Model T was different from any other car that had been made before. It not only looked different from

other cars, but it was made with a new kind of customer in mind. From the start, it had been designed as a practical and reliable means of travel for ordinary people—the people whom Henry Ford called "the great multitude."

Despite what the advertisement said, the Model T was not a handsome-looking car. Ford's design made no concessions to style. Nor was it powerful. It was a no-frills mechanical workhorse for everyday use. This, Ford believed, was what people were waiting for.

The Model T went on sale on October 1, 1908. That day saw the achievement of a ten-year-old dream for Henry Ford. Over the next nineteen years, until the Model T finally ceased production, it also fulfilled the dreams of millions of farmers and small-town families across the United States who wanted a cheap, reliable, all-purpose means of travel. Commercially, the Model T was the most successful car ever made. More than fifteen million were sold worldwide. This was almost as many as were sold during the same period by all other car manufacturers together.

Two dates in July

Henry Ford was born on July 30, 1863, on a farm at Greenfield, near Dearborn, Michigan, about nine miles from Detroit. He was the eldest of six children in a family of four boys and two girls. His parents had immigrated to the United States from Ireland almost twenty years before.

For such families, life was a struggle. Henry's father, William Ford, was more successful than many Michigan farmers, but he had earned his success with endless hard work. He owned some primitive horse-drawn machinery, but in those days, much of farming was still grueling physical work.

The year and even the month of Henry Ford's birth were significant ones in American history. For two years, the United States had been fighting the Civil War. More than half a million men died before the struggle between the Northern and Southern states was over. Although the Civil War dragged on until 1865,

Henry Ford (above) was born on July 30, 1863, just weeks after the Battle of Gettysburg (below) began. Industrialization thrived once the war ended and contributed to Ford's later success.

Railroad workers pose for a camera as they build a cross-country line. The first railroad line to link the East and West Coasts was completed in 1869.

July 1863 saw one of its fiercest battles, Gettysburg. More than six thousand men died there, but it proved to be a turning point. The Southern army, commanded by General Robert E. Lee, was forced to retreat, and from then on, there was no doubt that the North would eventually win the war. The United States, instead of being two groups of warring states, would become united again. The changes that came with reunification indirectly contributed to Henry Ford's later success.

America grows

The Civil War created a huge demand for uniforms, firearms, and munitions, and that resulted in fast and efficient production. After the war, the manufacturing skills developed to cope with this demand were turned to peaceful purposes. At the same time, railways had begun to open up the undeveloped states of America's West. In 1865, work began on a project to link the East Coast states by rail with the West Coast. The line was completed four years later.

Two other significant industrial developments took place around the same time. The open-hearth

process of steel production was developed, which made the production of high-grade steel easier and cheaper than it had been before. Then, in 1865, the world's first oil pipeline was laid in the Allegheny River valley in Pennsylvania. This made it easier to move oil from the wells where it was collected to the industries that used it.

Alongside these industrial developments there was a huge growth in farming. The great corn and cattle lands of the West were opened up by the railroad. Over the next fifty years, hundreds of thousands of settler families—many of them immigrants from Europe—moved westward to set up their homesteads. These families and their children formed an important market for the products of American industry—including Henry Ford's cars. The foundations of the United States's future were laid.

Machine mad

Growing up on a remote Michigan farm, Henry Ford knew little of all this. He soon showed signs, however, that he belonged to a new generation of Americans interested more in the industrial future than in the agricultural past. Like most pioneer farmers, his

During Ford's lifetime, manual farm labor became less common, and the whole process of farming was changed by the use of machines.

• •

"Even when I was very young I suspected that much might somehow be done in a better way. That is what took me into mechanics—although my mother always said that I was a born mechanic."

–Henry Ford, from *My Life and Work*
• •

father, William, hoped that his eldest son would join him on the farm, enable it to expand, and eventually take it over. Henry proved to be a disappointment in that respect. He hated farm work and did everything he could to avoid it. It was not that he was lazy—far from it. When given a mechanical job to do, such as mending the hinges of a gate or sharpening tools, he set to work eagerly. It was the daily life of the farm and its repetitive tasks that frustrated him. "What a waste it is," he wrote years later, as he remembered his work in the fields, "for a human being to spend hours and days behind a slowly moving team of horses."

Henry was excited by the possibilities of industrialization. Developments in technology could free farmers like his father from wasteful and boring toil. During Henry's boyhood, however, these developments had hardly touched farming at all, and most farmers still did things by hand. Low profits, the uncertainties of the weather, and farmers' instinctive resistance to change meant that none but the richest and most far-sighted farmers were willing to take advantage of the new age of machines.

So Henry turned his attention elsewhere. When he was twelve, he became very interested in clocks and watches. With fascination, he peered into the workings of a timepiece and watched the movement of ratchets, wheels, springs, and pendulums. Soon, he was able to repair clocks and watches for friends, working at a bench he built in his bedroom.

Breaking away

Henry had never gotten along well with his father. Not one to show his feelings, William Ford seemed interested in his son only as a helper on the farm. In Henry's eyes, his father had wasted his life in remorseless hard work for little reward, and Henry did not intend to repeat the pattern. Henry's mother, Mary Ford, was a more loving influence.

From his parents, Henry learned to love the countryside and understand it through careful observation. Mary also taught him, by example, the virtue of thrift,

Mary Ford, Henry's mother, died when he was young.

a lesson that stayed with him all his life. For farming families like the Fords, thrift was often the key to survival. Henry was brought up to hate waste, dislike any kind of luxury, and regard hard work—provided it produced results—as life's main purpose.

In 1876, Henry suffered a grievous blow. Mary died in childbirth. There was now no reason for him to stay on the farm, and he resolved to get away as soon as he could.

Around this time, steam engines joined clocks and watches as objects of Henry's fascination. According to an account given by Henry himself, he first saw a steam-powered vehicle in 1877 when he and his father, in their horse-drawn farm wagon, met one on the road. When the driver stopped to let the wagon pass, Henry jumped down and bombarded him with technical questions about the engine's performance. From then on, Henry became infatuated with steam engines. At the age of sixteen, he took a job at a Detroit workshop that made and installed them.

Moonlighting

Henry stayed with an aunt during this time and worked at the steam engine workshop during the day. In the evenings, he moonlighted as a watch repairer—

"He had, from childhood, an impelling urge to make things; to take materials and turn them into something that moved, or into tools that helped to make other things. That urge guided his whole life, and is probably ninety percent of the secret of Henry Ford's success."

—C. L. Caldwell, from *Henry Ford*

11

more out of interest and to fill his time than because he needed the money.

Over the next three years, he toyed with the idea of setting up his own business as a watchmaker, but when he worked out the costs and the likely market, he rejected it. He would need to make huge numbers of watches to keep the price down, but "watches were not universal necessities, and therefore people generally would not buy them." In those days, people did not need to wear watches. Clocks were displayed on public buildings such as town halls, churches, and factories. In farming districts, the sun provided all the timekeeping people needed. Henry's comment shows, however, that he already had in his mind the idea that made his fortune. If he could find a way to make cheaply enough something that everyone wanted, he would have the beginnings of a thriving business. To this, he later added a refinement—people do not always know what they want until they are told.

Meeting Clara

For the time being, however, Henry Ford's ambitions had to wait. In 1884, when Ford was twenty-one, his father gave him forty acres of timbered land to tempt him back to rural life. Ford accepted the offer, and for the next few years, he managed his property, ran a sawmill, and built a house with great energy.

During this time, Henry Ford met a local girl, Clara Bryant. Ford was not like any of the other young men with whom Bryant associated. He was rather serious and intense. He did not approve of drinking or smoking. It is said that he learned to dance only in order to be able to meet her. Such a pastime had not interested him before. Bryant found that she was attracted to Ford's intensity and enjoyed being involved in discussions of his business ideas and dreams. Romance blossomed, and on April 11, 1888, Henry Ford and Clara Bryant were married.

Once they had settled down, however, farm life began to bore Henry again. He had found a new technical interest. In 1879, a lawyer named George Baldwin

Selden had designed a motorcar that used a fuel engine. Selden was not an engineer and did not actually build his car, but he filed a patent so that no one else could copy his ideas unless they paid him a fee. This, however, did not stop others, both amateur and professional engineers, from experimenting with fuel-driven cars. News of their efforts was carried in the technical magazines that Henry Ford read avidly. Ford felt desperately frustrated and trapped on the farm, away from the city and the new developments taking place. At last, in 1891, he had had enough. In the late summer of that year, he and Clara loaded their furniture onto a wagon and left for Detroit.

Lawyer George Baldwin Selden (left) designed and patented the first full-powered motorcar.

Responsibilities

A chance meeting with an old co-worker led to a job for Ford as an engineer at the Edison Detroit Electricity Company, a leader in another new industry. Power stations were being built and cables being laid in most major U.S. cities; the age of electricity had dawned. Although Ford quickly mastered his new job—so quickly that within

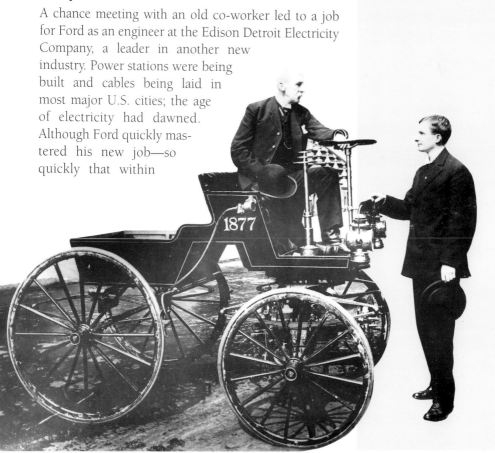

four years he was chief engineer at the Detroit power plant—his interest in fuel engines had come to dominate his life. At first in the kitchen of his home, and later in a shed behind his house, Ford spent his spare time trying to build an engine of his own design.

Meanwhile, his domestic responsibilities had increased. In November 1893, Clara gave birth to their first and only child, Edsel.

Learning the hard way

Ford learned the hard way what a slow, painstaking business it was to build an engine by hand from scratch. Every piece of every component had to be fashioned individually, checked and rechecked, and tested. Every problem had to be worried over and solved by the builder. To ease the burden, Ford joined forces with another mechanic, Jim Bishop. Even so, it was two years before they had built a working car. It was an ungainly looking vehicle, mounted on bicycle wheels and driven by a rubber belt that connected the engine to the rear wheels. Ford called it the "Quadricycle."

The first Ford on the road

The first trial of Ford's car, in June 1896, began with an anticlimax. He and Jim Bishop had worked through the night to get it ready for the road, and it was almost dawn before they finished. Rain was pouring down. They wondered whether they should put off the trial until daylight and better weather, but they decided they could not wait. They pushed the car up to the shed door only to find that it was too big to go through. Impatient and frustrated, Ford picked up an ax and began to demolish the front wall of the shed. So it was, at about 4:00 A.M., that Ford's first car made its maiden trip through the wet streets of Detroit.

The sight of "Crazy Ford," as he was known, driving about in his weird-looking vehicle, sometimes with his wife and son, now three years old, became a familiar one in Detroit. Already, Ford was thinking of improvements. To finance them, he sold his first car for $200 and started to build a second.

A fateful choice

Henry Ford was soon faced with a difficult decision. While he quietly built his car in the shed behind his home, the Edison company had taken no interest in his after-work activities. What employees did in their spare time was their own affair. Once Ford started to drive his car around, though, and once it was known that he had sold one car and proposed to build another, his employers began to wonder if he was giving enough attention to his day job. To put him to the test, they offered him a promotion to general manager of the Detroit plant—as long as he agreed not to tinker any-more with cars.

The promotion meant a big increase in his salary—enough to enable him to buy new tools and materials, rent a larger workshop, build an improved version of his car, and provide a better home for Clara and Edsel. The one thing that he would not be able to do was build another car. The young Ford family had to live, and no one who worked on his own could hope to make a living building cars. To become a carmaker, Ford needed partners, money with which to establish the business and buy tools and materials, and a regular income.

A decision is made

After ten sleepless nights spent worrying over this problem, Ford found backers and made his decision. With investments from a handful of local businessmen, led by a Detroit timber merchant, William Murphy, the Detroit Automobile Company formed in 1899. Ford, now thirty-six, resigned from the electricity company and became the new company's chief engineer. There was a price to pay, however. He had to take a cut in salary.

Storms over Detroit

Although Ford was by now adept at car engineering, he had little first-hand experience in the business world. Building cars in the evenings as a hobby took no real account of the costs of materials or manual work. Ford had been glad to get $200 for his first effort, but that

In 1896, Ford took his new invention, the Quadricycle, out for one of its first road trips.

was nowhere near the car's real value in terms of his time and skill. He knew nothing about the complex process of how to price a manufactured product. He needed to take into account materials, hours of work, and overhead such as rent and power. Above all, he needed to earn a profit so the investors in the company could be paid and so he could expand the company's business. His limited experience with these things made running a business difficult.

Another problem was Ford's personality. He was an individualist who found it difficult to work with other people. Unless his business partners or employees agreed with him completely, he believed they were against him. Business decisions, though, are often a matter of compromise; different options have to be weighed

against one another and then one must be chosen. Successful businesses can stem from the foresight, talent, and determination of a single person, but their survival usually depends on a number of people working together with a common sense of purpose. Ford believed that he was always right. If pushed, he simply ignored evidence that conflicted with his own ideas.

For their part, his backers were impatient. Fifteen months went by. Only a handful of cars had been produced, and the company was heavily in debt. At last, the other directors' nerve broke. In November 1900, they closed the company, sold its materials, parts, and equipment for scrap, and fired Henry Ford. He did not attend the board meeting to hear the decision. "If they ask for me," he told a colleague, "tell them I had to go

• • • • • • • • • • • • • • • • • •

"Every generation has its own problems; it ought to find out its own solutions. There is no use in our living if we can't do things better than our fathers did."

—Henry Ford, 1925

• • • • • • • • • • • • • • • • • •

A modern Ford race car zooms along a track. Motor racing was one of Henry Ford's early interests. In 1901 he became the American motor-racing champion.

out of town." If there was one thing that Henry Ford could not bear to hear, it was the suggestion that he had failed.

It was the lowest point yet in Ford's life. He had no job. He had, though he may not have admitted it even to himself, failed the Detroit Automobile Company. He could not afford to keep a home for his wife and son, so the family went to live with his father, now retired from the farm and living in Detroit. Clara began to worry about her husband's health and the family's future.

A new venture

Ford rebounded, though. Within a few months, he had persuaded five of the investors in the failed Detroit Automobile Company to back him in business again.

The men opened the Henry Ford Company, and they planned to design and build a racing car.

There is some mystery about this phase of Henry Ford's life. His story, years later, was that he really wanted only to produce a low-priced car for the "great multitude" but built racing cars instead because that was what the other directors wanted. The directors' story was the exact opposite. Whatever the truth, the racing cars that Henry Ford built were certainly successful. Driving one of them, he became the American motor racing champion in 1901. Three years later, another Ford racer broke a world record. It traveled one mile in 39.4 seconds at a then-incredible speed of 91.4 miles per hour.

The Henry Ford Company lasted for sixteen months until, once again, Ford had a disagreement with his

Henry Ford prepares to drive one of his company's racing cars. Ford's racers proved to be very successful.

partners. The partners continued with the company and chose a new name, which became famous at the luxury end of the motor industry—Cadillac. Meanwhile, Ford continued to build racing cars in partnership with a young racing cyclist, Tom Cooper, who had made a fortune in prize money. This alliance, too, ended quickly. Henry Ford had begun to look like bad news. He may be a brilliant mechanic, it was said, but he just could not get along with people.

Ready-to-buy

While he worked on his racing cars, Ford, now approaching forty, had also been thinking. By the early 1900s, there were plenty of engineers who were able to produce a working car for customers to order. What if, Ford wondered, rather than wait for rich customers to place an order for a car, a manufacturer were to mass-produce cars that could be bought off the shelf in the same way that people bought other things? While he struggled to master the mechanics of car-making, Henry Ford considered this idea and began to shape his vision of the car industry of the future. By 1903, his ideas were clearly formed. This industry would lure customers into showrooms rather than wait for them to call. It would offer them cars they could drive away then and there. It would make the ownership of a car so attractive, even essential, that every family would want one. By building cars in large numbers, it would be possible to bring down the price to a generally affordable figure. Also, if cars were produced in mass numbers, Ford's aim of buying off the shelf would be achievable.

These were revolutionary ideas in the motor industry of the time. Twenty years had gone by since two German engineers, Gottlieb Daimler and Karl Benz, had independently produced cars powered by a fuel-driven engine. Both had set up companies that produced cars commercially and, within a few years, had granted licenses to manufacturers in other countries. The motor industry that had developed around Daimler and Benz's companies produced cars for the rich, though. Each car was hand-built by highly skilled

• •

"Ideas are of themselves extraordinarily valuable, but an idea is just an idea. Almost any one can think up an idea. The thing that counts is developing it into a practical product."

—Henry Ford, from *My Life and Work*

• •

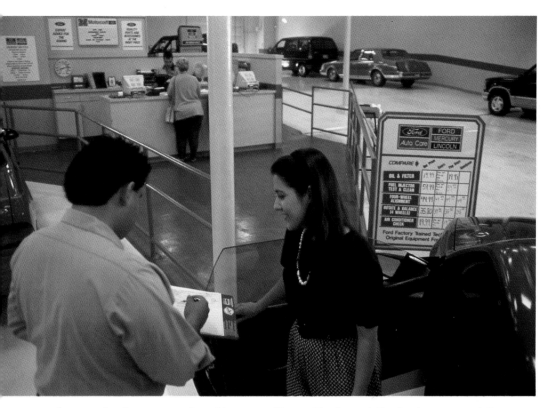

craftsmen, in the same painstaking way Henry Ford had built his first models. Ford's dream, on the other hand, was to make every family a motoring family.

A Ford sales representative consults with a customer. Henry Ford recognized that a good relationship between dealer and customer was vital to business success.

The rules of business

Experience had taught Henry Ford an important lesson. To build cars was one thing, to sell them another. For most of the population, cars were for other people—fast cars for the young, stately cars for the rich. The trick was to make everyone realize that motoring could be for them too.

In other words, the idea of car ownership had to be marketed. A generation earlier, Isaac Merrit Singer had, by clever marketing, persuaded hundreds of thousands of American women that a sewing machine was an essential piece of equipment for every home. It was true that a motorcar was a far more complex and more expensive product than a sewing machine, but the same principles could be applied.

When the Ford Motor Company began in 1903, James Couzens (below) joined as its general manager. Henry Ford (opposite) started as vice president.

So, Henry Ford combined his ideas for volume car production with his growing realization that the public must be tempted, even persuaded, to buy. As shown by the example of other products made by mass production, prices would be progressively lowered, thereby making the product accessible to even more customers.

Another discovery Ford had made, however, was that financing volume car production was more complex than he had anticipated. Almost all the costs are up front. In other words, they have to be paid before a single car is sold. A factory must be built or rented. Money must be spent on design and testing. Tools and equipment must be bought. Materials must be obtained, and workers must be paid. This was the problem that had put the Detroit Automobile Company so heavily in debt; large sums of money were spent, but only a handful of cars produced.

A new beginning

By 1903, Henry Ford had built up a reputation around Detroit, but it was not a good one. He had fallen out of favor with three sets of backers. He was obstinate and self-regarding. Rather than stay and complete a troubled project, he walked away.

There was one man in Detroit who had faith in Ford, though. He was the city's leading coal merchant, Alexander Malcolmson. He had been impressed with Ford's racing cars, and in 1903, he suggested that they form a company, with a handful of Malcolmson's business associates, to produce a commercial automobile. The new car would be designed for sale to the growing number of everyday motorists, rather than to racing enthusiasts. On June 16 of that year, the new company—the Ford Motor Company—was born, with Malcolmson as president and Henry Ford as vice president. One of the smaller shareholders was Malcolmson's accountant, James Couzens, who joined the Ford Motor Company as its general manager and played a key role in its early history.

Almost at once, a dispute broke out between Ford and his new backers. He wanted to produce the new car entirely in-house according to his own design, with the company making all the parts. In order to put a product on the market quickly, and get some of their outlay back, the others wanted the car to be assembled from parts brought in from outside. Couzens could be just as obstinate as Ford, and the latter idea finally won.

This stock certificate (left) shows Henry Ford's original investment in his company.

Connections abroad

The first Ford cars were built from the chassis, or the base frame, upward by teams of two or three mechanics who worked on a group of four cars at a time. Stock runners brought parts from the warehouse as they were needed. For the skilled mechanics, there was a lot of stooping and stretching, which slowed down the work. They also had to wait around while one operation was finished before they could move on to the next.

As he watched all this activity on the factory floor, Ford began to realize that there must be a more efficient way to build cars. Waiting around wasted time and money, an idea that offended the principles of thrift Ford had learned all those years ago on the farm.

So Ford tried to improve factory production. He decided to assemble the cars on stands or benches that

could be moved along from one team of workers to the next. This increased efficiency and productivity, but the cars were still largely hand built. At that time, there was no other way to organize car assembly. There were no standardized parts, so each car had to be built individually.

Despite these problems, in its first year, the Ford Motor Company managed to build more than six hundred of its Model A cars. Model A was followed by improved versions—B, C, F, K, N, R, and S—as Henry Ford struggled for better performance and reliability. (The missing letters represent experimental models that never reached the production stage.)

Within months of the founding of the Ford Motor Company, the Model A attracted attention from abroad. Barely six months after the company was established, two Model A cars had found their way across the Atlantic to Great Britain, where a man named Percival Perry had acquired the right to sell Ford cars for the next five years. International demand grew for the company's products, and by 1904, Ford's Model A had been exported to Canada and Australia. In the same year, Ford Motor Company itself established a base in Canada.

A dream of the future

A self-taught engineer, Henry Ford was unable to read an engineering drawing. He worked by instinct and claimed to be able to tell whether a part was well designed by holding it in his hands. This, however, held up progress and was a source of frustration to his partners and colleagues. The cost of each car rose so that as one Ford model succeeded the next, the price began to creep up to the luxury car level. Among luxury car makers, there was fierce competition, and Ford had little to offer that other manufacturers could not do as well or better. Indeed, compared with some of the splendid cars that were now produced, Ford's cars looked dull and cumbersome.

Once the Ford Motor Company started to become established, Henry Ford returned to his dream: to make a car for the "great multitude." His vision was of

a plain, down-to-earth, no-nonsense vehicle that could cope with the rough, rutted roads of America's farming states and even bump over dug-up fields without trouble. With this in mind, the car needed to have higher clearance from the ground than most cars of the time. It needed to be simple enough technically to be repaired and maintained by farm mechanics with everyday tools. It needed to be cheap and had to last, as farmers expected their equipment to do. These criteria laid the foundation for the Model T.

Without waiting to discuss the idea with Malcolmson or the other directors, Ford announced his plan to the Detroit newspapers in the spring of 1905. He would, he said, build ten thousand cars to sell at $400 each. Not surprisingly, there was dismay and anger on the board of the Ford Motor Company. Yet another split was inevitable. By quick and ruthless wheeling and dealing, Ford bought out the directors who were opposed to his plan, including Malcolmson. By November, he owned 58 percent of the company's shares, which gave him control of its activities. James Couzens, however, stayed.

At last, Ford had achieved an ambition that he had

Ford restored the farm where he was born in Dearborn, Michigan, and built an old-world village around it (opposite). His company's world headquarters (above) is also located in Dearborn.

nurtured since his departure from the Detroit Automobile Company. Then, as he wrote in his autobiography, "I resigned, determined never again to put myself under orders." He had to break that pledge in order to survive in business, but now, finally, he was in a situation where he could make all the decisions.

"All Ford"

Ford lost no time in revealing his plans to the press. He wanted to gain the interest not only of the public who were his intended customers, but also of businessmen in small towns across the United States who might want to become local Ford dealers. His new car would, he said, be "all Ford." This meant that every component would be supplied from within the Ford factory. This would not be the existing factory in Detroit where the company had started out, but a new one to be built on a sixty-acre site on the old Highland Park racetrack just outside the city.

Outside the first Ford Motor Company showroom, Henry Ford posed at the wheel of one of his Model T cars.

Then Ford gave his promise: "I will build a motor car for the great multitude. It will be large enough for the family but small enough for the individual to run and care for. It will be constructed of the best materials, by the best men to be hired, after the simplest designs that modern engineering can devise. But it will be so low in price that no man making a good salary will be unable to own one—and enjoy with his family the blessings of hours of pleasure in God's great open spaces."

The most surprising thing about Ford's announcement was that he planned to make only one model. Later, he announced an even more restrictive decision. He said, "People can have any color they like, as long as it is black." This was against the business opinion of the time, which argued that people wanted choice and would not buy a product that did not offer it.

Developing a network

Between 1905 and 1907, with the help of a small team of engineers, Ford, now in his forties, worked away single-mindedly at the design of the new car. He also supervised the making of a half-scale model. This was tested, taken apart, put together again, and tested once more. A full-scale prototype, or trial model, followed. Ford tried it out on a hunting trip to Wisconsin with two of his engineer colleagues. They covered 1,357 miles on sixty-eight gallons of fuel, driving about twenty miles to the gallon, which in those days was considered very economical. The Model T behaved well in this trial, and Ford ordered that his new factory should prepare for full-scale production as soon as it was ready. At the same time, through advertisements and press interviews, he introduced his new car to the American public.

Ford test drove the first Model T (above, top) himself. Today, monitors and sensors test new cars for technical performance, safety, and comfort.

27

French (top) and
American posters
advertised Ford cars.
By 1913, Ford had
sold cars in many
countries around
the world.

The Ford logo

The 1908 advertisement listed ten branches in the
United States and one each in London, Paris (where a
sales branch was established that year), and Toronto,
where the Model T could be inspected and ordered.
This was only the beginning, however. Henry Ford
wanted to make it as easy for rural Americans to buy a
Model T as a new pair of boots. The heart of his marketing plan was to set up a network of dealers, local
businessmen with a building that would serve as a
showroom, who would tie themselves exclusively to
the Ford name and sell only Ford cars. The plan was
that within the next five years, there was to be a Ford
dealer in every American town with a population of
more than two thousand. Visibility was vital to sales. As
soon as the Ford Motor Company had been established, the distinctive Ford logo, which has altered very
little since then, had been devised. Simple and unmis-
takable, short and memorable, it was another valuable
marketing tool that gave Ford cars and the showrooms
of Ford dealers a special character.

"The world on wheels"

Henry Ford did not confine his ambitions to the North
American continent, but continued to build on the
international links that had already been made. By
1910, as dealer networks were set in place within the
United States, Ford cars had reached Japan, Spain, and
the Austro-Hungarian Empire.

The first Ford factory outside the United States was set
up in Manchester, England, in 1911 as a result of a growing demand for Ford's Model T. In the first year, more
than three thousand were built. A French Ford assembly
plant opened in Bordeaux in 1913. It began to look as if
one of the early Model T advertising slogans—"the car
that put the world on wheels"—was no idle boast.

"Tin Lizzie"

It was not long before the Model T acquired affection-
ate nicknames. Among the most memorable were the
"Tin Lizzie" and "The Flivver." These were the first of

many jokes made about the Model T, but Henry Ford did not mind. He quickly realized that the jokes were free advertising. Although Americans joked about Tin Lizzie, they still bought it. Ford's masterstroke had been to design a car that was suitable for the rough and rocky conditions of rural America. At that time, the best roads outside towns and cities were dirt roads with a two-inch layer of gravel on top of the bare earth. Away from these, the roads were mere farm tracks. With its high clearance and rugged construction, the Model T was unsurpassed at coping with these conditions. What was more, the design of its engine was so simple that a farmer or a farmhand with basic mechanical knowledge could handle breakdowns.

Sales of the Model T during its first year reached 10,607 at $850 each. Each year until 1913, production in the United States almost doubled the previous year's. The rest of America's carmakers could only look on with a mixture of astonishment and envy.

The problems of success

It was good to have a runaway success, but Henry Ford worried about those customers who could not be supplied. Many of them, he knew, would go to another make of car and possibly stay with it forever. In the case of farmers, they might just buy another horse instead.

The success of the Model T also created two other problems. One was that the Ford Company had become the victim of the success of its own promotion. The second was that the first Model Ts were still practically hand built, a painfully slow method for a product in high demand.

Mass production

The breakthrough that solved this problem was the assembly of cars by mass production methods. Henry Ford is often thought of, wrongly, as the father of mass production. He was the first manufacturer to apply it to car assembly, but mass production itself

The 1925 Model T (below) looked a lot like the 1908 version. The lack of change in design made later models seem old-fashioned.

was an industrial method whose use had been growing in the United States for more than one hundred years.

It began in 1798 with a firearm manufacturer, Eli Whitney, in New Haven, Connecticut. He was given an urgent U.S. government order for ten thousand muskets. In those days, it was usual to make each gun by hand as a piece of craftsmanship, but the order was too large and too urgent to be handled in that way. Whitney built machines so accurate that they could duplicate the separate parts of the muskets identically. Rather than painstakingly fit the parts of each individual gun together and make tiny adjustments until they worked smoothly, muskets could be assembled quickly from interchangeable parts. There was an added bonus in this. If, in use, one part broke or was damaged, it could easily be replaced by an identical part from stock.

The U.S. Army was wary of Whitney's ideas, but he proved his point by assembling a musket at high speed from piles of assorted parts in front of the generals' eyes. Other gun manufacturers were quick to adopt Whitney's idea of interchangeable parts. During the nineteenth century, mass production spread to such industries as clock and watch making and to the manufacture of sewing machines, typewriters, and bicycles. Compared with the assembly of a car, however, these

Ford's mass production system (above and right) required that parts be delivered to the appropriate section of the production line, promoting efficiency. Even in today's factories (opposite), Ford's principles of mass production still apply.

were relatively simple devices, and all could be moved easily from one workbench to the next. Mass production in the motor industry was a great challenge.

Taking work to the worker

The first principle of mass production, Ford wrote, is that "the work must be brought to the man, not the man to the work." The moving assembly line was Ford's way to achieve this, but the idea was established long before Henry Ford was born. As early as 1738, an American miller, Oliver Evans, had devised an early form of the assembly line. He used a chain of buckets to carry grain through his mill. The grain started out in its raw state but ended up sealed sacks of flour at the end of the chain.

The importance of timing

The idea of accurately timing manufacturing operations—another essential feature of mass production—came from yet another American engineer, Frederick Winslow Taylor. He was a pioneer of what he called "scientific management." Taylor's theory was that productivity could be dramatically increased if the minute details of each operation carried out by a worker were observed and every movement made was noted. This allowed operations to be simplified by, for example, placing materials and parts in the most convenient position to eliminate wasted effort and time. Taylor found that if the average time taken to carry out a particular task could be observed, the cost of the time spent on each task could be built into an accurate estimate of the total cost of the work. The time could also be used to fix rates of pay for different tasks. Taylor's ideas were hugely attractive to Ford. He incorporated many of them as he planned the mass production of cars at the new Highland Park, Michigan, plant.

Getting it together

The separate techniques of manufacturing that make up mass production came together gradually after Highland Park started producing cars. It took about

seven years to reach the point where each operation was brought into the mass production process.

Ford hired an efficiency expert, Walter Flanders, who arranged for the work to be subdivided into twenty-nine separate, small operations, called sub-assembly

This 1914 photo depicts workers on an assembly line at the Highland Park plant.

lines. Flanders stationed a group of unskilled workers who had been trained only to perform their particular tasks at points along a conveyor. The workers did not move; they simply added their part as the incomplete engine moved past them on the conveyor. This saved time. Flanders then moved from department to department, assessed the tasks, divided them up, and set up sub-assembly lines for each component.

Meanwhile, experiments were carried out on a main assembly line. In the first one, two men dragged the chassis of a Model T through the factory with a rope, and workers added parts as it moved along. The next experiment replaced the men with a horse and windlass. The results were impressive. The time taken to assemble a complete car fell from about twelve and a half hours to just under six.

According to Ford, there were three principles that contributed to the success of mass production. He described these as the planned, orderly movement of the product through the factory; the delivery of work to the worker; and the careful analysis of manufacturing operations. It was important, too, that the work be delivered to the worker at waist height to eliminate the bending and stretching that were so wasteful of time and energy.

Value for money

The effect of the introduction of mass production at Highland Park was dramatic. In 1913, the number of Model Ts produced was 168,220, and in 1914—the first year of full assembly line operation—it had increased to 248,307. The time required to assemble a Model T fell steadily until it reached an unprecedented ninety-three seconds. This was not good enough, Ford said. He wanted to produce a car every minute.

These production changes were accompanied by a steady fall in the price of the Model T. Each drop in the price, Ford well knew, brought more potential customers into the market. "Every time I reduce the charge for our car by one dollar," he claimed, "I get one thousand new buyers." He had beaten his own promise, made back in 1908, to offer Americans a car for only $400 as Model Ts reached the low price of $260.

Supply and demand

The scale and speed of the Ford operation soon revealed flaws in the assembly system. Some suppliers could not keep up with the pace of Ford's demand for parts. As a result, deliveries became erratic and there were holdups on the production line because parts had not arrived. Secondly, in their haste to keep up, some suppliers neglected their inspection procedures. Ford found that it was impossible to impose quality control

· ·

"The car of the future must be a car for people, a car that any man can own who can afford a horse and carriage; and mark my words, the car is coming sooner than most people think."

—Henry Ford, 1910

· ·

standards on suppliers in their own factories, so Ford inspectors had to reinspect deliveries and reject defective parts. The delays that resulted from all of this were resented by the time-conscious, value-for-money-conscious Henry Ford, and he began to set up plants to make his own parts.

Over the first few years of the Model T's production life, an increasing proportion of parts was made in Ford factories. This left only special items to be brought in from outside the company. The Ford Company became what is known in today's management language as a vertically integrated business, in which as many manufacturing processes as possible were carried out under direct company control. Ford's goal to produce parts in-house was finally within his grasp.

Automobile production plants, like these two Ford factories, tend to be built outside cities where land is plentiful and cheap. This is because mass production methods require large work sites.

The loss of a business partner

As the new assembly lines were installed, Henry Ford's business manager and colleague since 1903, James Couzens, was closely involved with any problems within the work force. Couzens and Ford, who almost came to blows over Ford's earlier wish to produce all Ford parts in-house, were both highly ambitious men. Both were also jointly responsible for the success of the company. The two men, however, disagreed over crucial business decisions and plans.

The final break came over the men's different ideas about the role that Ford plants should play in the war efforts of World War I. In 1915, James Couzens left the company, declaring that he could no longer work alongside Henry Ford. He was later bought out of the company by the Ford family. His $900 investment made in 1903 had grown to a value of more than $29 million.

A new president

In 1919, a newcomer took over the Ford Motor Company. He was Henry Ford's son, Edsel. Now twenty-six, Edsel became the company president. He had been brought up to expect that he would one day take his father's place as president of the Ford Motor Company. Edsel Ford and his wife, Eleanor Clay, already had a first son, Henry II, to continue the Ford line in the Ford Motor Company.

Edsel's appointment did not mean that his father was to decrease his own involvement in the company, however. Henry Ford himself had already become something of a folk-hero to the American public—the story of a poor farmer's son who had brought everyday motoring to the "great multitude."

A generation gap

Henry Ford continued to govern his company closely. His concern for his workers extended to their lifestyles. He used internal publications to impress upon them how they should live their lives.

This paternalistic style of management had been fairly common in the nineteenth century. Employers

often provided libraries, entertainment, reading rooms, and education and sports facilities for their workers. Although Henry Ford did not go that far, he did do several things. He set up good training facilities (a tradition that the Ford Company has maintained). He established a hospital for Ford workers, and he went to some lengths to encourage outstanding young employees who caught his eye. Such paternalism was out of date in the twentieth century, though, especially after the social upheavals of World War I, which had made so many people—young people in particular—question the values of the previous generation.

River Rouge

Despite the changes brought about by the war, the popularity of the Model T grew. Demand had outstripped the resources of the Highland Park factory,

and a completely new plant opened in 1919 at River
Rouge, six miles southwest of Detroit. This plant had
large docks, railway yards, storage for coke and ore,
blast furnaces, coke ovens, and a foundry that covered
thirty acres, which was at that time the largest in the
world. Coke and ore arrived at River Rouge by ship and
train. Steel was made and cylinder blocks, crankshafts,
and other Ford parts were cast on the same site.

The site where Henry Ford built the River Rouge
plant was chosen carefully because of its potential to be
self-sufficient and self-serving. The Detroit, Toledo and
Ironton Railway ran through the site, however. So,
Henry Ford bought the railroad because its right of way
interfered with his plans. He was a man who would not
be thwarted once he had made up his mind.

Economy of scale

With the Model T's popularity ever increasing, it was no
wonder that the car was so hugely profitable. The Model
T was a perfect example of what is known in business as
economy of scale. Any new product that hits the market—the video, the compact disc player, even a new
medicine—is expensive at first because all the costs of
research, design, testing, and tooling up for production
have to be paid for. If the product flops—as many do—

those costs still have to be paid. If the product succeeds like the Model T, though, the manufacturer can begin to reduce the sale price as sales rise and the initial costs are absorbed. With only minor changes, the Model T was in production from 1908 to 1927. The vast American market had enabled Ford to expand into Europe— still with the same car—and undercut any price that European manufacturers could offer. There was even, in the 1920s, a drive to sell Model Ts in the post-revolutionary Soviet Union, despite the United States's opposition to the Soviet Union's Communist regime.

Zapping the dealers

To reach these expanding markets, Henry Ford had built up an extensive dealer network. The relationship between manufacturers and their distributors is a com-

Above: The Kremlin in Moscow. In the 1920s, the Soviet Union became an export outlet for Ford cars.

Left: A prototype of any new product, whether it is a CD or a new model of car, is an important step in the production process.

plex one of mutual dependence; each side relies on the other. The dealer has to face the customer and is in the first line of fire if there is anything wrong with the product. The dealer has to rely on the manufacturer to deliver on its promises. In turn, the manufacturer has to rely on the dealer to push the products and explore all the possibilities of sales within the area. The success of the Model T had made very good profits for the small-town businessmen who obtained Ford dealerships. It was in the small towns of the midwestern and western United States that the Model T had its greatest triumphs.

39

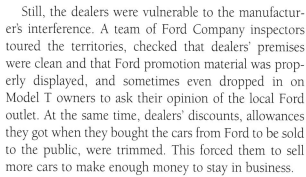

Opposite: The Ford logo advertises the company from atop a factory building. Henry Ford always believed in the power of advertising.

Below: This Colorado Ford dealership used a catchy slogan to attract customers duing the 1950s.

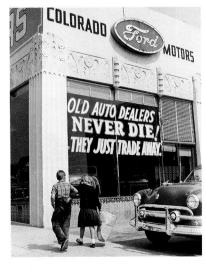

Still, the dealers were vulnerable to the manufacturer's interference. A team of Ford Company inspectors toured the territories, checked that dealers' premises were clean and that Ford promotion material was properly displayed, and sometimes even dropped in on Model T owners to ask their opinion of the local Ford outlet. At the same time, dealers' discounts, allowances they got when they bought the cars from Ford to be sold to the public, were trimmed. This forced them to sell more cars to make enough money to stay in business.

In 1920, an economic depression hit the United States, which threatened the future of the Ford Motor Company as it threatened other prominent American companies. Henry Ford needed cash quickly and borrowed heavily from the banks to stay in business. Of all the factors in business, cash flow is one of the most vital. A company can be doing very well in theory, but unless there is a steady stream of money from sales, the company's debts to suppliers of parts and materials and interest payments to the banks cannot be paid. This was the situation Henry Ford faced. Under the weight of the depression, sales figures plummeted. The flow of orders from customers to dealers, and from dealers to the Ford Company, began to dry up.

A business decision

Ford's response was an astonishing piece of business strategy. The Ford factories continued to turn out Model Ts at their usual pace, and these were sent out to dealers whether they had been ordered or not. When the dealers protested, they were told that unless they paid cash on delivery for the cars and paid the delivery charge, they would be removed from the Ford dealer network. This would, of course, have meant ruin, so they were forced to take out bank loans to pay the Ford bill. In this ingenious but ruthless way, Ford transferred his own bank debts to the dealers.

A change in fashion

In 1923, with one car built every ten seconds, Model T production hit a peak of 2,011,125, four and a half

times the sales of the United States' second best-selling car, General Motors' Chevrolet. Because Ford had concentrated for fifteen years on one model, with only minor changes from year to year, the company had been saved the expensive design and retooling costs that some rival car manufacturers, who believed in the need for a new model or at least a new look each year, had suffered.

As almost everyone in the Ford Company recognized, except for Ford himself, times were changing, however. The Model T's time was up. Sales figures in 1925 told the story. Other manufacturers reported increased sales, but sales of the Model T fell by sixty thousand. Henry Ford, now sixty, still refused to accept the inevitable. No matter how much pressure the Ford Motor Company put on the dealers, though, sales continued to fall. In 1926, Model T production slumped by half a million. The United States now had its second generation of motorists, young people who wanted something more exciting than the workhorse their parents drove. That something was the Chevrolet—the

"Chevy"—whose sales figures, though still a long way behind Ford's, had begun to creep up on the Model T's.

Refinements and accessories

The Chevy's appeal was not only that it had a younger image. It was also better equipped. The buyer of a Model T got a basic car to which accessories, such as an electric starter and wheel trims, had to be added. The Chevy, on the other hand, came complete with these and other refinements. What was more, a Chevy buyer got a car that had been designed in the past year or two. The Model T design had hardly been changed since 1908.

Ford dealers came to Detroit in great numbers to plead with Ford to replace the outdated model. A last-minute attempt was made in 1926 to breathe new life into "Tin Lizzie" by reducing its ground clearance and making it available in "fawn grey, gunmetal blue, phoenix brown and highland green." Eventually, though, Henry Ford accepted the truth that the Model T had come to the end of its useful life. On May 31, 1927, the 15,007,033rd and last Detroit-built Model T came off the assembly line at River Rouge. Production continued for a few more months at Ford's European assembly plants in England, Belgium, and Italy, but the company had finally said good-bye to the car that had made it successful. The big problem was, of course, what would follow the Model T.

Never the same again

The Tin Lizzie's successor was the Model A. Different from the Model A first introduced in 1903, its completely new design incorporated many of the features that rival manufacturers, who had taken advantage of Henry Ford's resistance to change, had already built into their cars. These included four-wheel brakes (the Model T had brakes on only two wheels); hydraulic shock absorbers, which made use of a piston inside a cylinder of oil to smooth out the ride over bumpy road surfaces; and the use of safety-glass for the windows.

The Model A sold well—production began with an order of 727,000—but it had nothing like the success

In 1927, competition and a fall in sales caused Ford to stop production on the Model T.

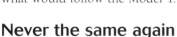

"**We do not make changes for the sake of making them, but we never fail to make a change once it is demonstrated that the new way is better than the old way.**"

—**Henry Ford**, from *Ford in Europe*

of Tin Lizzie. The Chevrolet and a newcomer from Plymouth continued to challenge Ford in the North American market. In Europe, competition was even fiercer, with the French companies Peugeot, Citröen, and Renault, the Italian Fiat, and the British Austin and Morris companies all fighting for a significant place in a growing market. Ford would remain a leading player in the motor industry, but it would never again be able to claim undisputed leadership in the popular car sector.

French car manufacturer Renault advertises its product. Renault was one of the companies that challenged Ford sales in Europe.

A union ban

Henry Ford had proved that he was a determined businessman. He had intended to achieve his vision of the car industry and let nothing stand in his way. Where unions threatened to disrupt his work force, he banned them from his factories.

Unions are organizations of workers who join together to protect workers' rights. Ford did not want this sort of organization to work within his business. He argued that, since he came from humble origins himself, he knew what was best for his employees. Despite U.S. laws that authorized unions in industrial plants, Henry Ford held out against them. The Ford work force was denied the protection from exploitation that it badly needed. There was instant dismissal for any worker who could not keep up with the pace of the assembly line. Talking, unless it was essential to the work, was forbidden.

Mass production and stress

The dramatic changes in the way the Ford Motor Company was set up in terms of the day-to-day work on the assembly line caused inevitable problems. Changes in the way people are expected to work produce tensions among a company's work force. This was seen in the 1970s and 1980s with the introduction of computers into almost every aspect of working life, which resulted in the loss of many jobs and the retraining of millions of other workers. The same had been true a century before Henry Ford's time when steam-operated spinning and weaving machines replaced hand-powered processes, and thousands of workers in the textile industry had to learn new skills or face unemployment. The switch from hand assembly to mass production in the car industry brought similar stresses.

Craftspeople who built cars from start to finish in small groups could take pride in their work. They had the satisfaction of seeing the car they had assembled as a team roll out of the workshop. They could also relate to each other as individuals, valuing their own and their teammates' skills. The assembly line robbed workers of these compensations. It was hard for a worker to take any pride in what he or she did or obtain any satisfaction from it if his or her only function was to fit a nut to a bolt that would be tightened by the next worker down the line.

When the textile industry switched from hand assembly to mass production, workers had a difficult time making the adjustment when the skills required of them changed.

The meaning of work

Such changes caused great concern in the industrial
world of the 1920s and 1930s about the increased
meaninglessness of people's working lives as so many
old craft skills were replaced by unskilled machine
minding. This ran alongside concern about the changes
that occurred as large numbers of people left the countryside to find better-paid factory work in the cities.
Henry Ford could be classed as a tough and sometimes
insensitive employer, but he could hardly be blamed for
the tide of social change that was sweeping across the
industrial world. The decline of traditional crafts and
the rush of people to the cities had been going on for
more than a century. The car industry simply reflected
trends that were already established in other industries.
Ford also was not slow to point out that when farm
workers gave up their jobs and came to Detroit to find
work in his factory, they showed no signs that they
wished they were back on the farm.

There were other disturbing aspects of work on the
assembly line, however. In a small engineering workshop, employees were able to work, within reason, at
the pace they chose. It was true that a foreman might

come and tell them to work a bit faster, but at least he was a human being with whom the worker could reason. On an assembly line, the speed of the main assembly track dictates the pace of work. The individual worker has no control. If production needs to be increased, the assembly line can be set to travel faster, and this can be a source of stress and discontent. When Ford workers saw Henry Ford announce yet another cut in the price of the Model T, they knew perfectly well that it had been at least partly achieved by their having to do more work for the same money.

The inevitable explosion came in 1937 when members of a union called the United Automobile Workers of America planned to hand out membership leaflets one May afternoon as Ford workers came off their shift. That day proved to be one of the blackest days in the history of American workers, and it was one that was not easily forgotten.

Following page: Ford created a separate company to make tractors specifically for the small farmer. The Fordson was an instant success.

The battle of River Rouge

The union men took up their position on a footbridge that linked the River Rouge factory with a bus stop. They were met by members of a Detroit street gang, hired, it was said, by the company, who warned them off. Protesting, the union members left but ran into another gang of hired heavies who began to beat them up. Press photographers at the scene had their cameras snatched and their film destroyed, but enough of them escaped to expose the scenes of violence in the following day's papers.

Over the next few weeks, there were similar scenes at other Ford plants. The company's treatment of the unions and of Ford workers became a national scandal, and the government's National Labor Relations Board issued a stern warning to Ford. Eventually, Henry Ford gave way and allowed unions into Ford factories.

Below: Violence broke out at the River Rouge factory when employees protested their working conditions.

Broader horizons

The automobile industry was no longer the same business that Henry Ford had helped to shape at the

The Fordson major

beginning of the twentieth century. So, he began to spread his interests in other directions. He tried, unsuccessfully, to take a controlling interest in a hydroelectric power project. He set up an aircraft production company. He built a model village and museum to celebrate his own background, and he even took up an interest in traditional square dancing, with a full-time dance instructor and a band on the payroll.

Independently of the Ford Motor Company, he set up a company to make tractors specifically for the small farmer. The Fordson, as it was called, became an instant success and repeated on a smaller scale the triumphs of the Model T.

Father and son

Edsel Ford's presidency had continued to be very much overshadowed by his father. Even so, Edsel remained loyal to both Henry Ford and the business. He visited European plants and enforced business plans. By 1934, the Ford Motor Company had assembly plants in France, Belgium, Italy, Great Britain, Germany, and Spain. In 1943, however, the Ford Company suffered a blow. At age forty-nine, Edsel died from stomach cancer.

The United States was then two years into World War II and relied heavily on Ford plants for the production of military vehicles and aircraft. Edsel's son, Henry Ford II, Edsel's natural successor, was in the U.S. Navy. In Henry Ford senior's view, there was only one man who could step into the presidency—himself.

By this time, the Ford Motor Company was at the lowest point in its history. The eighty-year-old Henry Ford, despite his continuing enthusiasm, no longer had the strength to manage the company. There were real fears that it might collapse.

Opposite: Henry Ford's grandson Henry Ford II (standing) poses with company vice presidents Benson Ford (seated, left) and William Clay Ford (seated, right). Henry Ford II became president of the Ford Motor Company in 1945.

Below: During World War II, Ford plants manufactured tanks and aircraft.

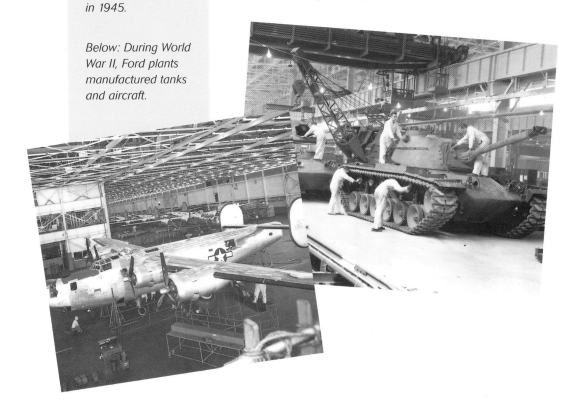

As he resumed the presidency of Ford, Henry was underestimating the power of two strong women, his wife, Clara, and Edsel's widow, Eleanor. Eleanor, who had inherited Edsel's shares of the company, now had voting rights in the business. Between them, the two women arranged for Henry Ford II to be released from the navy and then began to campaign for the elder Henry to hand over the presidency to his grandson. It took two years to get him to agree. Finally, in 1945, Henry Ford II became president, and his grandfather stepped down for the last time.

Father of the motor industry

On April 7, 1947, Henry Ford died at his home in Dearborn. At the time of his death, the power was out, and his house was lit by kerosene lamps and candles, a scene similar to that of his birth eighty-three years earlier.

It is no exaggeration to say that few men have changed people's lives as dramatically as Henry Ford did. He was born into a world where most travel was still dominated by the horse and where steam-powered travel was a wondrous new invention. His technical understanding, which was phenomenal considering that he was entirely self-educated as an engineer, enabled him to grasp the new technology of the internal combustion engine and improve its performance.

A vision that was completely his own inspired him to apply the new technology to the needs of the people he knew best and from whence he came. They were the "great multitude" of ordinary folk with whom he grew up and whose lives he believed could be made easier and more satisfying by mechanization. The often-quoted

One of Henry Ford's main goals was to make cars available to everyone. Partly because of this, people's lifestyles have changed. Traffic jams, interstates, and drive-through restaurants now dominate the American landscape.

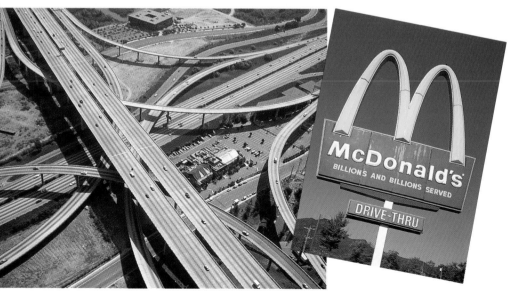

claim that Henry Ford "put the world on wheels" is absolutely justified. His contribution to the industrial and social life of the twentieth century was unique.

Bringing Ford back to life

The company that Henry Ford II inherited in 1945 was in bad shape. In the United States, it had concentrated mainly on war production for four years, to the neglect of its commercial markets. In continental Europe, many of its factories had been shattered by air raids or battle. Those that stayed in production were also geared to war work. In countries such as Great Britain, there was a desperate postwar shortage of all kinds of raw materials, and the supply of new cars lagged well behind demand. Throughout the Ford factories in the

This 1946 poster advertised a new Ford car. After World War II, the company tried to reestablish the interest of its large, loyal customer base through national and local publicity.

United States and Europe, research and development had been interrupted by the war, and when car production resumed, it was of models that had been introduced in 1939 or even before.

Added to this, in Europe, a problem was posed by the way Ford's European operations had developed piecemeal, or bit by bit, country by country. The result was that some European companies actually competed against each other in the same markets with rival dealer networks. This was a waste of corporate, or company, energy and robbed Ford in Europe of the chance to produce large numbers of cars for the continent's many markets.

The Model T's legacy

Despite these problems, the years of prosperity with the Model T had given the Ford Company the power and confidence to fight for its place in the market. It had a huge customer base that dated back nearly twenty years, made up of people who had never owned any car but a Ford. The loyalty of Ford owners was carefully nourished by national and local publicity. In addition, there was still room for expansion, for Ford and its rivals, in the United States and overseas.

Henry Ford II was only twenty-eight when he became president. He was well aware of his inexperience. Some of the years he would normally have spent learning the business had been taken up by war service.

His solution was to bring in an experienced team to support him. The newcomers were from outside the car industry. They were "new brooms," university-trained professional managers, who questioned every one of the Ford Company's long-standing business methods.

A climate of change

By the mid-1970s, it was clear that the entire automobile industry was in a state of change. Competition was commonplace. There were too many manufacturers, including relative newcomers from Japan, chasing too few customers. This led to cooperation in joint product development between rival companies. For example, Ford of Europe developed production links for certain models with Volkswagen of Germany and with the Japanese carmaker Nissan. In America, Ford built up an association with the Japanese Mazda Company. These links produced cars that were identical in engineering terms but were given distinctive names,

Japanese dealers show off a new Ford Mustang. Rather than fight its competition from Japan, the Ford company cultivated business relationships with Japanese carmakers.

Three popular Ford models —the 1908 Model T, the 1934 Model Y, and the 1992 Escort—show the extensive changes in car design that have kept Ford ahead of its competitors.

badges, trim, and accessories by the partner companies, which marketed them individually. One example of such a car was the Ford Mondeo, launched in 1993.

The modern motor trade

The structure of the motor industry was not the only way in which the motor trade changed. Every step in the production of a new car, from the earliest design stages to final assembly and testing, was revolutionized by the computer. Drawing boards, on which teams of designers produced drawings of thousands of individual car parts, were replaced by screens on which designs can be made and modified at the touch of a light pen.

Ford engineers were able to exchange information with their colleagues around the world through a database system that the company developed independently. The "Worldwide Engineering Release System" was believed to be the world's largest privately owned database network. It provided essential design information, which enabled engineers to call up working drawings to their computer terminals.

On the production line, computer-controlled robots perform many of the operations that were formerly done by hand or by workers who used hand-held machine tools. On the Ford Mondeo, for example,

· ·

"The competitive road ahead will be challenging. But I want to assure everyone that whatever comes our way, there will continue to be a Ford in your future."

—Ian Trotman, chairman of Ford, June 15, 1994

· ·

95 percent of the thirty-four hundred welds on the body shell were made using robot control.

With safety in mind

The budget for expenditure in new projects in the British market in 1993 was more than $3 billion. Research and development was an area of great concern to the company, both in terms of new products and the safety standards of the cars that made it to production. In the United States, Ford was one of the first car companies to start crash-testing vehicles. By 1994, technology had taken the place of some actual crash testing. Crashes could be simulated on screen and the type of damage assessed. Also by early 1994, airbags had become a standard safety feature on certain Ford models, including the popular "subcompact" car, the Fiesta.

Caring for the environment

Passenger safety aside, care for the environment was one of the company's oldest concerns. It stemmed from

Above: Today, most cars are designed on-screen.

Below: One of the first companies to crash-test its cars, Ford included airbags as a standard feature in some vehicles in 1994.

Henry Ford's own dislike of unnecessary waste and his interest in the countryside. Ford promoted recycling within his plants early on. By the 1990s, the Ford Company had begun to sponsor the worldwide Conservation Awards, run by the Conservation Foundation. These awards invited organizations to enter conservation projects into a Europe-wide competition.

In terms of the motorcar, a high polluter itself,

Ford spent much time and research investigating new ways to cut fume emissions. European regulations called for the fitting of catalytic converters to the exhaust systems of all new cars made since the early 1990s. Ford also investigated further measures that could be taken to reduce the pollution created by cars. The company even considered ventures such as electrically run cars. In addition, it has looked into producing cars that are more than 80 percent recyclable.

A world market

To eliminate the danger that it might become too fragmented as it had been in Europe between the world wars, the Ford Company decided to try to globalize.

In 1993, plans were put into motion to unite the production of Ford Europe and Ford America and ultimately, to link production worldwide. This was a new step forward. It meant that certain plants would be responsible for the production of particular models of cars for the worldwide market, not just for specific countries, as was the case before. Such a change would

Above: Ford cars are sometimes transported from the factory to the dealer by water. This cuts down on pollution.

Opposite: Henry Ford's interest in the countryside and his concern about waste influenced the company's way of doing business. He researched ways to cut pollution from car emissions and promoted recycling in his plants.

By continually adapting, the Ford company was as successful in the 1990s (top) as it was during the days of Model T production (above).

eliminate the duplication of designs, and make better use of resources. It would also allow the company to move toward a "single set of worldwide processes and systems in its product development, manufacturing, supply and sales activities." Such goals were not far away from Henry Ford's original dream. The Ford Motor Company had been an international company since 1903 when Henry Ford sold his Model A to Canada. Within ten or so years, the company was selling cars throughout Europe, the United States, and Asia. In 1994, Ford had plants or other facilities in thirty countries, sold cars in more than two hundred markets, and had a work force of nearly 340,000 people worldwide.

Timeline

1863 July 30: Henry Ford is born, in Dearborn, Michigan.

1876 Henry's mother, Mary Ford, dies in childbirth.

1884 Henry Ford returns to Greenfield to manage land given to him by his father.

1888 April 11: Henry Ford marries Clara Bryant.

1891 Henry and Clara Ford move to Detroit, and Henry starts work with the Edison Detroit Electricity Company. In his spare time, he begins to design his first car.

1893 November 6: The Fords' first son, Edsel Bryant Ford, is born.

1896 June: Henry Ford's first car, the Quadricycle, makes its first run.

1899 August 19: The Detroit Automobile Company is founded by William Murphy, with Henry Ford as its chief engineer.

1900 November: The Detroit Automobile Company closes.

1901 The Henry Ford Company is formed.
October 10: Henry Ford becomes American motor-racing champion.

1902 The Henry Ford Company closes.

1903 June 16: The Ford Motor Company is formed, with Alexander Malcolmson as president and Henry Ford as vice president. The Model A Ford is launched in the United States and exported to Great Britain.

1904 The First Model A is sold in Canada and Australia. The Ford Motor Company establishes a base in Canada.

1905 Ford announces the Model T to the American press.

1908 The Model T goes into production and sells in the United States, London, and Paris.

1911 The first overseas plant for the production of Model Ts is established in Great Britain.

1912 The first European Ford parts depot opens in Hamburg, Germany.

1913 The first Ford assembly plant opens in Bordeaux, France.

1915 James Couzens leaves the Ford Motor Company.

1917 Henry Ford II is born to Edsel and Eleanor Ford.

1919 A new Ford plant opens at River Rouge, near Detroit. Edsel Ford becomes president of the Ford Motor Company.

1926 Model T production slumps by half a million.

1927	May 31: Ford announces the end of Model T production. October: The last Model T is produced at River Rouge.
1937	May: Union protests take place at many Ford plants.
1941	The United States enters World War II, and Ford factories convert to war production.
1943	Edsel Ford dies of stomach cancer. Henry Ford again becomes president of the Ford Motor Company.
1945	Henry Ford II becomes president of the Ford Motor Company, and Henry Ford finally retires.
1947	April 7: Henry Ford dies at the age of eighty-three.
1959	The fifty millionth Ford vehicle is produced.
1976	Ford's new European small car, the Fiesta, is introduced.
1979	Ford establishes links with the Japanese motor company Mazda.
1987	Henry Ford II dies. Ford establishes links with the German motor company Volkswagen.
1993	Ford launches the Mondeo.
1994	The safety feature of airbags becomes standard in many Ford models, including the Fiesta. Nissan dealers agree to sell Ford cars in Japan.

Glossary

assembly line: An arrangement, in mass production factories, whereby machines and workers put together the parts of a product step by step as it travels through the factory.

commercial: Concerned with commerce, or the exchange of goods through buying and selling.

company: A group of two or more people registered to carry out a trade or business. A company is obliged to conform to certain regulations, which may vary from country to country or state to state.

consumer: A person who buys services or products; the customer.

general manager: A person who is elected to organize and lead a company. He or she is responsible for making critical decisions that will help the company achieve its business goals.

hydroelectric power: Electricity produced by waterpower.

innovative: New or creative.

investment: When money, time, or effort is put into something, for example, setting up a business or buying a house, in the hope that it will result in a profit in the long term.

investors: People who make a financial investment in a company.

manufacturer: A business or company responsible for the production of goods on a large scale, usually through the use of machinery.

market: In terms of a company's sales plan, the number of people who might want to buy a particular product; it also means to sell the product in an organized and preplanned way.

overhead: In business, general expenses, or costs that do not belong to a particular department, such as heating and rent.

paternalistic: Behaving in a fatherly way to other people.

pioneer: Someone who originates new ideas.

product: An item that is either manufactured or naturally created.

profit: The amount of money a company or individual has left over in a business venture after costs and expenses have been paid.

prototype: A model product that is used for testing so that necessary changes can be made before it is manufactured commercially.

recruitment: Seeking out new members to join a company.

share: An equal part of a company's assests, that can be bought and owned by a member of the company or shareholder who is then entitled to a percentage of the company's profits.

shareholder: Someone who owns shares in a company.

showroom: A room set aside to display the goods for sale.

windlass: A machine used for raising weights.

Index